ATLANT

Myths, Legends and History

KIV Books

Copyright © 2017

Copyright © 2017 KIV Books

All rights reserved. This book or any portion thereof may not be reproduced or used in any manner whatsoever without the express written permission of the publisher except for the use of brief quotations in a book review.

Disclaimer

This book is designed to provide condensed information. It is not intended to reprint all the information that is otherwise available, but instead to complement, amplify and supplement other texts. You are urged to read all the available material, learn as much as possible and tailor the information to your individual needs.

Every effort has been made to make this book as complete and as accurate as possible. However, there may be mistakes, both typographical and in content. Therefore, this text should be used only as a general guide and not as the ultimate source of information. The purpose of this book is to educate.

The author or the publisher shall have neither liability nor responsibility to any person or entity regarding any loss or damage caused, or alleged to have been caused, directly or indirectly, by the information contained in this book.

Table of Contents

INTRODUCTION 5

ATLANTIS ACCORDING TO PLATO 7

ATLANTIS IS THE MINOAN CIVILIZATION OF SANTORINI 13

ATLANTIS IN THE COAST OF SPAIN 19

ATLANTIS IS THE ISLAND OF MALTA 23

ATLANTIS IN THE ATLANTIC OCEAN 25

ANTARCTICA IS ATLANTIS 29

MINOR THEORIES ON ATLANTIS 31

ATLANTIS IN POPULAR CULTURE 39

ATLANTIS IN GREEK MYTHOLOGY 43

OTHER MYSTERIOUS CIVILIZATIONS THAT DISAPPEARED 45

CONCLUSION 49

Introduction

Atlantis – the mythical city that was first mentioned by Plato in his Timaeus and Critias. While largely believed to be fictional, Atlantis has made its way into literature and manages to flourish over the years. Through time, the myth became a legend that eventually enticed individuals to delve into this ancient city and find out whether Plato's references are mere fiction or actually a fact.

In this book, you will find out the various arguments to and for the existence of Atlantis as well as the various theories on where it is located, why it disappeared, and the civilization rumored to exist within this island.

You will also find out about the many theories surrounding the story of Atlantis and the islands thought to be what was left behind by this ancient civilization. You will learn of the characteristics of Atlantis as relied by Plato and how they have been used as a literal map in order to find this utopian society.

At the end of this book, you are encouraged to make your own conclusions about the famed Atlantis. Bear in mind that with frequent studies being made all over the world, there may be new discoveries that are not reflected in this book.

Atlantis According to Plato

"...in a single day and night of misfortune, the island of Atlantis dissapeared into the depths of the sea."

-Plato, 360 B.C.

Atlantis – a mythical island first introduced by Plato through his works Timaeus and Critias. Despite having such a small significance in Plato's writings, the story of Atlantis endures – perhaps because of its inherently mystical state. Today, scholars are divided on whether or not Atlantis actually existed. In this Chapter however, we will tackle Atlantis as it was told by Plato.

Introduction of Plato

It was during 360 B.C. that Plato introduced the story of Atlantis or the island of Atlas. It was widely believed that the fictional island is a representation of a rival by Ancient Athens. This theory is not questionable considering how Atlantis was introduced through an allegory on the hubris of nations, whereby Atlantis attacks Athens and the latter managed to repel the attack. Instead of one big island as portrayed in many movies and books however, Atlantis was made up of concentric islands. Moats separated each island with a canal running through the center, linking all the moats together. Atlantis therefore, appears to be more water than city with Atlanteans quite possibly using many boats to travel from one location to another.

The island was said to be bigger than Asia Minor and Libya combined. When the gods divided up the land, Atlantis went to the god Poseidon who named it after his son Atlas. It was also Atlas who became the king of the said city.

Location of Atlantis

The alleged location of Atlantis is a little vague as Plato simply says that it is "beyond the pillars of Hercules". This can be interpreted in various ways and thus the recurring debates on where the famed island is located. Many believe that it was in the Atlantic Ocean while others argue that it was in the Mediterranean Sea. Others say that it was in Europe while some authors cite other locations such as Antarctica.

When It Existed

According to Plato, Atlantis existed well before his time, approximately 9,000 years before 360 B.C. where he introduced the concept of the island to his followers. He even said that the story of Atlantis has been passed down from one generation to the next through priests, poets, and notable personalities. Note however that the only known record of the island is that divulged of Plato. No other reference to Atlantis was made before his time.

Plato's Alleged Source

According to Plato, the story of Atlantis was told to him by his grandfather. His grandfather, on the other hand, heard it from the statesman Solon who lived 300 years before he did. Solon heard it from an Egyptian priest. It is these little details that make people wonder whether Atlantis has some basis in fact.

The Civilization of Atlantis

Plato reveals that Atlantis was founded by demigods or half-gods and half-humans. It is a utopian civilization with advanced technology and possessing of a great naval power. It was said that they grew so powerful, Atlantis managed to conquer parts of Egypt, Africa, Europe and even Tyrrhenia which is known today as Etruscan Italy.

How It Disappeared

Atlantis sank down into the sea after the gods were displeased by it and its inhabitants. The theory is that the civilization of Atlantis grew too bold of their advanced technology and power, and thus the gods brought forth a natural disaster than sunk the island.

Of course, this is the mythical account of Plato and while scholars today cannot prove that a god caused the natural disaster, they can at least find out whether a natural disaster actually occurred.

The looming question however is: is it even possible for an entire civilization to be wiped out by a single natural disaster? A look in past events shows that it is indeed possible for an entire city to disappear just overnight. Volcanic eruptions have literally wiped out entire cities, not just killing its inhabitants but also burying the city in ash. In some locations where this catastrophic event happened, only the roof of houses can be seen after the eruption.

Hence, it can be said that it is indeed possible for an entire civilization to be wiped out overnight due to some form of natural disaster. Of course, there are currently some theories about Atlantis that are different from the circumstances laid down by Plato.

The 5 Characteristics of Atlantis Derived from Plato

With just 40,000 words, Plato managed to create a legend that has endured thousands of years and has lit the first of discovery among professionals and amateur scholars alike. Despite the 40,000 words used to discuss Atlantis however, Plato only gave 5 concrete descriptions of the famed island. It is these 5 characteristics that are being used by scholars today as a checklist to find out if theorized locations are Atlantis. Granted that there are many theorized locations that do not conform with these alleged characteristics, but those theories are based on the assumption that Plato somehow made a mistake in his predictions.

Still, here are the characteristics of Atlantis according to Plato:

Concentric Circles Connected by Waterways

Think of the city of Atlantis as a bull's eye or a dartboard. Waterways run through the diameter of the city as connecting waterways. This should be the general shape of the island for it to be considered as the lost city of Atlantis.

Elephants Roam

Plato also said that elephants roam Atlantis. Thus, any theorized location must have elephants in their land. However, it must be noted that after thousands of years, it's likely that the present Atlantis no longer has elephants due to extinction or some other natural cause.

They Sacrificed Bulls

Plato also mentioned the sacrificial of bulls in Atlantis. Signs or evidence of bull worship and sacrifice must be present.

It Contained Red, Black, and White Rocks

The land was mostly made of red, black, and white rocks. This should be the general geology of the land if it will be considered as the lost Atlantis.

It Sank due to a Tsunami or Some Natural Disaster

Lastly, the island must be located in a place where tsunamis or other natural disasters are known to frequent. There must be satisfactory evidence that the civilization was wiped out because of this natural disaster.

A Great Naval Force beyond Their Time

Plato mentioned that Atlantis held a great naval force, making them a formidable enemy during times of war. This has been interpreted as Atlantis having access to technology that is far beyond their time. Thus, when in search for Atlantis, archeologists often look for signs of intelligent life such as the use of arithmetic, the use of a written langue, creation of pots, pans, a water system, and various other leaps in their way of life.

It Happened 9000 Years Ago

Plato's timeline allows scientists to further narrow down the possibilities. Thanks to many studies done today, scientists now have a fairly good idea of the world's timeline and the things that happened even before the existence of modern civilization. While nothing is assured, scientists can now put forth an educated guess of what existed, what happened, and how certain landscapes looked like thousands of years ago.

Atlantis Interpreted

Of course, there's still the pervasive idea that Atlantis is nothing but a figment of Plato's imagination. One of the smarter brains of his era, Plato is deeply adept in presenting arguments that support his position and it is likely that the story of Atlantis was created with this thought in mind.

According to him, a war broke out between Atlantis and Athens. The citizens of Atlantis with their great naval forces already conquered parts of Libya, Egypt, and a portion of the European continent. Citizens of the conquered islands were turned into slaves by the Atlantean army. While Athens fought against Atlantis with the help of other cities in a joint alliance, the efforts failed and the other cities withdrew from battle. Plato however stated that Athens alone perceived and eventually vanquished the force of Atlantis.

In Platos' story of Atlantis, the city essentially stands as a utopian civilization that has everything it could ever want but still fell and sank into oblivion. Plato presented it as a great civilization with powerful naval forces that went against the Athenians in battle. In his story, it was interpreted that Plato tried to communicate the value of staying true to one's morals. Despite the extent of their power and influence, Atlantis fell down because it was morally bankrupt. In contrast however, Athens is a small force that worked towards doing and achieving only good things.

Atlantis Is the Minoan Civilization of Santorini

"Without memory, there is no culture. Without memory, there would be no civilization, no society, no future."

- Elie Wiesel

A largely accepted theory is that Atlantis actually refers to the Minoan Civilization which tragically disappeared due to a large tsunami that was triggered by the eruption of Thera. Following this theory, Atlantis would then be situated in the Mediterranean Sea, near the island of Crete. More specifically, the city of Atlantis is the island of Santorini known today.

Harmonized with Plato's Description

The main argument against Atlantis being the lost Minoan Civilization stems from the fact that it does not accurately correspond with the description given by Plato. More specifically, the time frame supposedly does not match since the eruption of the volcano Thera happened less than 9000 years ago. According to AG Galanopoulos however, one of the proponents of the theory, it is likely that there was an error in the translation of Plato's works. According to him, it was actually "hundreds" instead of "thousands". Following this theory, the famed island of Atlantis existed 900 years before Solon, around the 15th Century B.C. However, the error in translation changes more than just the timeframe of Atlantis. This would also mean that Atlantis is actually smaller than purported. This also changed the Pillars of Hercules. Instead of the Straits of Gibraltar, the Pillars may not refer to two mountains.

Minoan Civilization

The Minoan Civilization is a 100% legitimate society that existed during 2600 to 100 BC. Their rediscovery was fairly recent through archeologist Arthur Evans who made the introduction during the 20th century. Since they are the first of their kind in the continent of Europe, the Minoan Civilization is dubbed as "the first link in the European chain" by historian Will Durant. It must be noted that while the volcanic eruption of Thera and the subsequent tsunami are the widely accepted reasons for the disappearance of the Minoans, this has not yet been verified.

Mythology

It is important to bear in mind that while the Minoan Civilization actually existed, there have been stories that linked the island to mythology. This is the reason why some are still under the misapprehension that the Minoans never existed and were just part of Greek Mythology. In truth, the word "Minoan" was inspired from King Minos who governed the island for 9 years – according to Homer. The famous author of the *Iliad* also said that Minos is the son of the highest Greek deity, Zeus. Some speculate however that the word "Minoan" was actually inspired from the word Minotaur. The Minotaur was actually a monster gifted by Zeus to Minos in order to protect his city. Although not directly linked, the daughter of Minos named Ariadne, actually helped with the killing of the Minotaur together with Theseus who is the son of Poseidon.

Homer further described that Crete once had 90 cities, the capital of which is Knossos where a sector of the Minoan Civilization thrived. He described it as having a labyrinth where the Minotaur was kept. While the story of the Minotaur itself remains in legend, the city of Knossos was already discovered in Crete by Sir Arthur Evans.

Evidence of an Advanced Civilization

Atlantis Civilization has always been theorized to be advanced for their time and the Minoan Culture seems to fit the bill.

They were the first European Civilization to have a form of written language known as Linear A and Linear B. Unfortunately, Linear A has never been deciphered. Those written of Linear B were mostly of an economic nature or an inventory of goods. Thus, not much is known about the Minoan Culture through their writings.

It is proposed that the Minoan language became extinct during the Greek Dark Ages. There are those who believe that the Eteocretan language was developed for the Minoan language, but this was never confirmed. In Knossos, clay cups were recovered with ink remaining on the surface.

Evidence of trade was found between the Minoans and mainland Greece. Evidence suggests that Minoans were primarily engaged in Mercantile, and are heavily organized in their approach of business – making them one of the most advanced in their age. Numerous products are the subject of trade with the Minoans with saffron being one of their most popular products.

One of the more prominent evidence that the Minoans are an advanced civilization however would be the excellent engineering of their homes. Their structures have an aqueduct system and indoor plumbing that was not seen until the rise of the Roman Empire.

Bull Worship and Elephants

Among their amazing frescos and pottery, it can be seen that the Minoan Civilization practiced bull worship. In fact, there are remnants of bull skulls found in Santorini, showing that the ancient dwellers of the island saw bulls as an important aspect of their daily life.

While there are definitely bulls in Santorini however, there is no evidence that elephants once roamed this island. No skulls of elephants have ever been recovered in the area, thus defeating one of Plato's descriptions of Atlantis.

Geography of the Island

This is where things get interesting. Undoubtedly, the island of Santorini looks nothing like the concentric circle described by Plato. According to scholars however, the island was originally circular in shape. As it stands, the island of Santorini looks like an inverted letter C. Approximately 1400 years ago however, a volcano rested on the space in between the island, forming a semi-perfect circle of land mass. When the volcano exploded, the eruption was of such degree that it wiped out all the civilization residing nearby. Afterwards, the volcano crumbled into itself, causing the huge space seen today.

Unfortunately, no evidence of waterways can be found on the island, defeating its argument that Santorini could be the island of Atlantis with the Manoians being the Atlanteans according to the story of Plato. The rocks however are a proper match. Scientists have found that the colors meet Plato's description of red, white, and black.

Life and Death of Minoan Society

There appears to be a discrepancy between the stories of Homer and the discovery of Knossos. If Knossos is part of Atlantis – then why was a city found in Iraklion? This is because this theory does not see Atlantis as an island but as a Civilization. Thus, the particulars of this theory are that Atlantis can be found in Santorini and refers exclusively to the Minoans. Following this theory, it is supposed that even the Minoans living in the outskirts of Santorini were also badly affected by the eruption of the volcano.

The heaviest reason why people argue that the Minoan Civilization is actually Atlantis relies on the fact that the Minoans also vanished – virtually overnight. While it is well accepted that a volcanic eruption caused their disappearance, this is just a theory that has never been proven. Indeed, the volcano found in Thera erupted at the same time when the Minoans were known to exist.

There are two theories circulating as to how the volcanic eruption could have led to the collapse of the Minoans. First is if the volcano spouted so much ash that it choked all kinds of life nearby, including the Minoans. Second is that only little ash was spouted, but the volcanic eruption led to a tsunami that wiped out the civilization.

Both theories are probable considering how the eruption in Thera, now Santorini, was one of the biggest one in known history. It scored 7 in the Volcanic Explosivity Index. By comparison, the 1883 explosion of the Krakatoa and the 1991 explosion of the Mount Pinatubo only scored a 6 in the scale.

Atlantis in the Coast of Spain

"Science and technology revolutionize our lives, but memory, tradition, and myth frame our response."

- Arthur M. Schlesinger

One of the most persuasive arguments towards the existence of Atlantis is the theory that the ancient civilization can be found off the coast of Spain. The theory is so persuasive that there are actually scientists following this theory and exploring the considered location of the sunken city. Employing numerous tools of science, this hunt for Atlantis takes into account the various geographical changes that happened on Earth ever since the alleged existence of the island 9000 years ago.

Mud Flats in Southern Spain

What makes this theory beautifully unique is the fact that Atlantis is being searched for in a non-body of water. Instead, the lost city is believed to be under mud flats off the coast of Southern Spain. The theory is that the city was swept off by a tsunami, causing it to be buried under what are now mud flats. The mud flats are located in Dona Ana Park in Cadiz, Spain.

A Sighting from Space

The reason for their conclusion is based on a satellite image that shows what appears to be a submerged city that fits the description of Plato. The concentric circle connected by pathways in the center can be seen from space through the use of a high-tech satellite system although the city itself is said to be submerged in the marsh land. Looking much like a bull's eye, comparison to Plato's description of the fabled Atlantis shows that the image viewed through satellite has proportions that are very close to what was mentioned by Plato. Even more intriguing is the obvious triangular pattern in the center of the bull's eye, which is believed to be the temple built for Poseidon. This particular temple was also mentioned by Plato in his allegory.

Deep Ground Analysis

Of course, the concentric circle seen from space is just the tip of the iceberg in the quest to figure out whether this is really the resting place of the fabled Atlantis. Deep ground mapping, underwater technology, and radar were used to analyze what can be found deep under the marshland. Scientists noted the presence of minerals that support their theory than an ancient civilization can be found underneath the soil. One of the more notable items seen is a large supply of methane which is produced when organic material undergoes decay. It was argued that the presence of a large city underneath makes for an excellent explanation as to why methane can be found underground. Of course, it must be kept in mind that there can be other explanations for the existence of methane and other minerals under the soil. Combined with the satellite image and the long history of tsunami in the region however helps solidify the theory that this was once the location of the mythical city of Atlantis.

Cancho Roano

Cancho Roano is an archeological site said to be further proof of the presence of Atlantis in the marsh land. Located at Badajoz, Spain – Cancho Roano are essentially 'small cities' made of stone and slate. It is argued to be a "memorial city" according to Doctor Richard Freund, citing that this was possibly built by Atlanteans who survived the tsunami.

To support his theory, he cites that the memorial cities were built in the shape or design of Atlantis. Even the Temple of Poseidon located at the center of Atlantis was replicated in these memorial cities.

He further points out the presence of slates that were used in the building. Slates cannot be found in Badajoz, Spain – but it is abundant near the original location of Atlantis. The theory is that Atlanteans who survived the tsunami took the time to come back and take slates to their new location in order to make their memorial cities.

Diggings to Discover the Fabled Atlantis

Unfortunately, diggings are not yet possible to confirm the theories set forth by scholars. Water can be found beneath the marshland which would make digging incredibly expensive. By their estimation, Atlantis is deeper than the water hazard and thus would require special handling for it to be uncovered. Future exploration of the site however will undoubtedly add to the theories and hopefully make it possible for scholars to actually dig through and see if their theory is confirmed.

Unfortunately, due to the lack of actual access to the site, it cannot be confirmed whether this underground discovery corresponds with the description of Plato. It will take some time before scholars will know whether the find is indeed a city inhabited by people who worshipped bulls, who had elephants roaming in their lands, and who had rocks the color of black, red, and white.

Atlantis Is the Island of Malta

"The only eal voyage of discovery consists not in seeking new landscapes but in having new eyes"

- Marcel Proust

The island of Malta, officially known as the Republic of Malta, is one of the most prominent islands to be the focus of the myth of Atlantis. Even the Germans during World War II decided to take over Malta, believing that it is part of the famed island of Atlantis. Located along the Mediterranean Sea, this island country is found in Southern Europe and has a population of just 450,000, more or less.

Arguments for Atlantis

Many believe that Malta is part of the famed city of Atlantis as many of the island's characteristics correspond with the description of Plato. To start off, Malta is home to architectures that seem to be advanced for their era. These architectures make use of rocks that weigh several tons each, putting into question the likelihood that an advanced civilization created these structures. Made even before the time of the Great Pyramids, these architectural wonders remain standing Malta today and is a frequent tourist landmark.

The architectures also display carvings by those who first built them. From here, evidence of animal sacrifice can be concluded. In particular, bones, bullhorns and images of bulls being sacrificed can be seen from these carvings, not to mention the actual bones that can be located at the site. This is akin to the description given by Plato about the Atlanteans.

Present Malta however, does not contain any elephants. Clearly written in Plato's account of Atlantis however, is the presence of elephants roaming the land. Still, an explanation was given by scholars regarding this matter. While Malta today has no elephants, evidence suggests that thousands of years ago, the island was home to elephants due to the presence of elephant fossils in the land. The theory is that years ago, Malta was connected to another island. Over the years, the island disconnected and the elephants that were left in Malta eventually died out.

Further underlining the argument that Malta is Atlantis would be the likelihood of a tsunami happening near the island. As per Plato's account, a great natural disaster sank Atlantis in a single day and night.

Of course, the question now is: why is Malta above water? If the island is the Atlantis Plato is talking about, then it would make sense for Malta to be below the sea instead of above it. There are several possible explanations for this.

First are the changing sea levels. While Malta may have been wiped out after a tsunami, the intervening years could very well cause the island to resurface. The Malta today could have gone under and come back in between Plato's time and today.

Another explanation is that only part of Malta succumbed to the tsunami instead of the whole island. This reasoning is support by the fact that off the coast of Malta, temples can be found underwater. These temples are remarkably similar to the ones found on the island. Thus, scholars believe that these temples were once part of Malta that eventually sunk down due to the tsunami.

Contradictions with Plato

Unfortunately, the characteristics of Malta do not fully match up with the accounts of Plato regarding Atlantis. While Malta presents bull worship, the presence of elephants, and the likelihood of a tsunami, the other characteristics are not present. The rocks found in Malta are of the wrong shade and no waterways can be found connecting the island. In fact, the island itself does not match the concentric circles as described by Plato. Furthermore, the temples were dated and it was found that they are only 5,000 years old.

Atlantis in the Atlantic Ocean

"Be open to ideas and thoughts you disagree with. It will unleash a debate in your mind and soul"

- James Kirk Bisceglia, Ancient Treasure

Being largely accepted as fictional, it's not surprising that there are varying opinions on the location of the city of Atlantis, when it was present, the civilization that lived there, and how it perished. While the version of Plato is more or less definite in the fate of Atlantis, the mythology of this island gave scholars carte blanche to create their own interpretations and definitions of Atlantis. In popular culture, Atlantis is also often used by authors, movies, and television shows, essentially muddying the waters on what is 'real' as per described by Plato and which ones are completely imagined or are deviant from what Plato has described.

The main debate however focuses on the actual location of this mythical island as well as the people who lived here. For the most part however, "Atlantis" is used as a collective word for any lost prehistoric civilization with advanced intelligence and technology.

Mid-Atlantic Island

The general consensus is that Atlantis was located in the Atlantic Ocean, just past the Strait of Gibraltar. It must be remembered that according to Plato, the City of Atlas can be found just beyond the Pillars of Hercules. Present scholars are of the opinion that these pillars are actually the Strait of Gibraltar and thus have been using the location as a compass to help them locate the sunken island.

Plato's own contemporaries were skeptical about the existence of Atlantis. Aristotle actually joked about this, citing Plato for his ability to create and sink an entire island out of thin air. Thus, further writings about the famed city are practically nil and it took centuries before Plato's references to Atlantis were once again expanded.

Reintroduction of Atlantis

Atlantis was not repeated again until the year 1627 when a novel titled "The New Atlantis" was published by Francis Bacon. A respected scientist and English philosopher, he depicted Atlantis as a utopian civilization which is both politically and scientifically advanced.

The theory was reintroduced in 1882 through the book "Atlantis, the Antediluvian World" by Ignatius Donnelly. It is this version of Atlantis that is currently being expanded in the 21st century.

The most prominent part of Donnelly's argument is that the Atlanteans were responsible for handing down accomplishments to ancient civilization. He theorized that disciplines like langue and farming were known to the Atlanteans – being a highly advanced civilization – and they managed to teach this to a population that would eventually become the ancestors of the present generation.

Donnelly is known as the man who really fanned the flame of the Atlantis myth. Prior to his book on the subject, the idea of Atlantis was practically buried in history until he took the idea and ran with it. One of his more prominent arguments includes the similarity of the pyramids found in Egypt and Central Africa. According to him, this suggests that a common ancestor taught these ancient civilizations how to create the stunning architecture. Following this theory, he suggested that it was survivors of the Atlantis that spread across the world and managed to spread their knowledge of an advanced civilization before dying out.

Busting the Theory

Donnelly's theory was perfectly serviceable at the time when it was put forward. He argued that the island was flooded due to the shifting waters of the ocean, sinking it so that it eventually disappears. However, science marches forward, causing better understanding on the ocean tides and plate tectonics, thus making Donnelly's theory improbable. While the science no longer backs up this theory however, there are still many whole believe that the island of Atlantis can be found in the depths of the Atlantic Ocean where Plato said it was located.

Theory on the Bermuda Triangle

Some scholars expanded on the theory of Donnelly by citing the possible connection between the Bermuda Triangle and the city of Atlantis. Also found in the Atlantic Ocean, it was theorized that the Bermuda Triangle swallowed up Atlantis and that the island was originally located in the area where the Bermuda Triangle now resides. One of the proponents of this theory was Charles Berlitz who is a well-known author of books dealing with the paranormal. According to him, the Bermuda Triangle could be the one responsible for the loss of the Atlantis, citing that the triangle is also responsible for the loss of ships and aircrafts passing through it or above it. Further evidence was given in the form of what seems to be man-made walls along the coast of Bimini. Later studies however show that these are natural rock formations.

Antarctica Is Atlantis

"I think part of the appeal of Antarctica is experiencing some sort of power, the foces of the natural world"

- Jon Krakauer

Antarctica also drew the attention of scientists, making it to be the lost city of Atlantis while others claims that Atlantis is actually hidden beneath all the ice found in Antarctica.

In a book written by Charles Hapgood in 1958 titled "Earth's Shifting Crust", it put forward the theory that 12,000 years ago, the crust of the earth shifted, causing one large island to move from its location into the area where Antarctica now resides. Due to the change in the position, the climate on this island also changed, forming all the ice that can be seen on the continent. Hapgood argues that before the shifting occurred, the island actually had a temperate climate and thus ideal for human life.

During such time, the island is home to an advanced civilization that eventually perished when the cold weather became extreme. The Atlanteans were eventually buried under the ice so that there's virtually no sign of their existence anywhere nowadays.

As science moves forward however, the theory of a shifting crush became less and less likely. It must also be noted that land movement through water will be a slow process and therefore unlikely to wipe out an entire civilization. This is also contrary to the accounts of Plato that in a single day and night, the city of Atlantis perished.

NASA Discovery

Further fuel was thrown into the fire however when NASA detected large structures underneath all the ice in Antarctica. Some of these structures are so tall and wide that they're rumored to be even bigger than the Eiffel Tower. Enthusiasts who are in search of the

Atlantis see this as possible evidence that the great continent was once the home of an ancient civilization. Some groups see this as evidence of waterways or conduits hidden beneath all that ice. Scientists who made the discovery however are a bit more skeptical about this theory and prefer to err on the side of caution. While everyone believes that this part of Antarctica deserves more study, it's unlikely that this is the lost city of Atlantis based on the evidence currently available.

Minor Theories on Atlantis

"A myth is an image in terms of which we try to make sense of the world"

- Alan Watts

Plato is well known for his intelligence and his brilliance. While choose to see his brilliance as an added evidence of the existence of Atlantis, others choose to see this as his clever way of sending a message with a hidden meaning or as a metaphor. Some scholars therefore are of the strong opinion that Atlantis did NOT exist, BUT that it was used as a representation of other events that actually happened.

Minor theories on the location of Atlantis have been put forward over the years, but very few were backed up by legitimate archeological findings. Proceeding on the theory that Plato somehow got his description wrong, Atlantis has been purportedly 'discovered' in places as far as the Americas, Sweden, Asia, Africa and the Middle East. In fact, you can point at any location in the map and you can guarantee that someone has put forward the theory that Atlantis can be found somewhere nearby. Such is the strength of this myth.

Following are some of the theories as to the existence of Atlantis that were heard but weren't given much weight.

Atlantis and the Black Sea Flood

One of the most popular theories along this line involves the Black Sea Flood. It was said that the loss of the Atlantis was inspired by the Black Sea flood which occurred during 5600 B.C. The Black Sea was then a small lake until the Mediterranean Sea rose, breaching Bosporus and eventually the Black Sea. When the flooded lake reached civilization, residents had no choice but to quickly move away from the location. By doing so, they've also spread tales of why they had to leave so quickly from their homes. Future retellings may have inspired Plato's reference to Atlantis.

Atlantis as the Garden of Eden

Religion has also taken a stab at theorizing the mythical city of Atlantis and what it contains. According to Christian theologian Kosmas Indikopleustes, Atlantis was actually the site of the Garden of Eden. The same theory was also put forward by Donnelly in his book, but this has been discarded by modern scholars.

The theory that Atlantis is the Garden of Eden is already the most prominent mention of Atlantis in terms of religion. While Christians, Jews, and Hebrews have all mentioned Atlantis in one form of another, few have accorded it such a high significance in their faith. In many cases, Atlantis was simply likened or used for comparison purposes.

Atlantis as One of the Major Theories for Being

There are those who use Atlantis as a possible reason for how men developed from scavengers to something of a more sophisticated sort. Scholars believe that there must be an event that turned man into a more intelligent being, using fire and essentially making the developments known today. While Atlantis is not seen as the "missing link", it is theorized that the knowledge that propelled man to a higher status came from them.

As per scholars, it stands to reason that Atlantis is a highly advanced population that taught non-Atlanteans of modern technology which was eventually passed on through the generations. While this theory may explain the current civilization, it still does not explain exactly where Atlantis came from.

Atlantis in Cuba

Another theory is that Atlantis used to be located near Cuba. This was theorized when purely by accident, a sonar machine managed to detect the presence of large formations more than 100 feet underwater. Since it is too deep for diving, the researchers had to resort to sonar and underwater cameras to help them figure out what the structures happen to be.

A rough estimate of what the structure looks like shows a city-like setup that looks a lot like the Mayan Civilization. It is estimated that there are pyramids existing underwater which could be a sign that this used to be a great city. Due to the depth however, it became impossible for further exploration.

Other than the structure themselves however, there are no other compelling evidence convincing experts that this is the lost city of Atlantis. There are no artifacts or physical evidence that points to any characteristics described by Plato. Experts are also skeptical of the city due to the fact that it is too deeply located underwater. For the most part, cities found buried beneath the sea are just 100 feet deep or less. The only reason why it can get this deep would be for an unnatural event such as the movement of tectonic rocks.

Atlantis in Support of Germany

During World War II, Germany also undertook a project in search of Atlantis. It must be remembered that the Germans were trying to prove that they were the master race during the War. Hitler believed that if they were the ones who find the lost city of Atlantis, then this will only prove their claims. One of the locations they fought hard to obtain was the island of Malta in the Mediterranean. Fortunately, this small island managed to stand against Germany and deflect its troops. In modern times, Malta is one of the islands that is theorized to be the actual island of Atlantis.

Atlantis Are Aliens

Another popular theory – although holding very little credence – is that Atlantis is a city established by aliens. Another version of the same story is that Atlantis is an ancient civilization that had contact with aliens and learned from their extraterrestrial advanced technology. Another theory also related to the extraterrestrial supposes that Atlantis did not sink but was lifted off.

Island of Pharos

Due to its location that somehow corroborates with that given by Plato, the Island of Pharos was said to be the mythical island of Atlantis. The theory was put forward through The Greek Myths produced by Robert Graves in 1955. He argues that this was the case before the island was connected via a causeway to Egypt during the time of Alexander the Great.

Greece

Robert L. Scranton published an article in Archeology, arguing that Atlantis can be found in Lake Copais. Later discoveries found a Mycenaean-era drainage complex in the area.

Somewhere Near Cyprus

American architect Robert Sarmast argues that Atlantis actually lies under the Mediterranean Sea, possibly somewhere along the Cyprus Basin. According to him, sonar data shows that there are man-made structures at the bottom of the Cyprus Basin which could be the monuments of the lost city. He points out that Cyprus also contains copper which meets the colored rocks described by Plato. Furthermore, there were dwarf elephants roaming the island.

Bahamas

The support for Bahamas being the site for the island of Atlantis relies on the existence of the Birmini Wall or the Birmini Road. This is a series of smooth rectangular rocks laid down side by side so that it appears to create a road. The road measures around 0.8 kilometers and appears to be manmade due to the smoothness of the surface. Enthusiasts who have found the formation believe that it used to be a wharf that an ancient civilization used for water travel.

Further proof is the presence of another manmade structure along the top portion of the island of Bahamas. According to enthusiasts, the topmost location of the structure makes it an ideal fort where an ancient civilization may have set up to protect their city against intruders.

A psychic by the name of Edgar Cayce also referenced Atlantis in 1923, predicting that the city will rise again in 1969. He further stressed that Atlantis is powered by a form of energy crystal. With the Birmini Road discovered in 1968, followers of Cayce believe that this is the Atlantis predicted by the psychic.

However, some scientists argue that the Birmini Wall is actually made of natural rock formations. Although they may seem unnatural and highly irregular in appearance, it has been known for nature to create such smoothly paved rocks.

Other than the presence of these structures however, there is no other evidence supporting the theory that Bahamas used to be the site of Atlantis. Most of the theories are unsupported such as the possibility of the civilization being wiped out by a tsunami caused by the falling of a meteorite near the sea. Studies also show that no humans lived in the Bahamas until 1000AD which means that the Birmini Wall could not be manmade.

1870s Mysticism of Blavatsky

Before Cayce made his predictions about Atlantis, there was the Russian Helena Petrovna Blavatsky, one of the proponents of the

Theosophical Society. They are often pointed out as the founders of what is currently known as the New Age movement. In 1888, Blavatsky agreed with the conclusions of Donnelly but added her own interpretation of what really happened to Atlantis and the people who lived here. In her book *The Secret Doctrine,* the mystic claimed that Atlanteans were the "Fourth Root Rate" as part of an ongoing racial evolution. She further alleges that the Atlanteans were succeeded by a present Fifth Race which is far superior due to the natural advantages brought on by evolution. Interestingly enough, she claims that the Fifth Race is her own race which is Aryan.

Furthermore, the mystic through the Theosophical Society alleges that Atlantis destroyed itself. Accordingly, an internal warfare occurred amongst the Atlanteans due to their use of supernatural powers.

Europe

There are also several theories stating that Atlantis is actually located in north of Europe, Sweden, and the North Sea. The place of Doggerland has also been cited as a possible location because it was flooded by a tsunami sometime during 6100 BC. This somehow corresponds with one of Plato's descriptions that Atlantis was sunk by a natural disaster.

Doggerland

Located below the Southern North Sea, Doggerland was said to be flooded around 6500 to 6200 BC. A geological study of the area shows that this strip of land is vast, covering the same space as the strength of Netherland, Germany, and the east coast of Britain. Theories abound that the area was originally home to humans, quite possibly with a rich ecosystem that promoted the growth of both plants and animals. As the sea levels rose, Doggerland started to sink under the water, leaving its inhabitants without a home. It is interesting to note that vessels have managed to drag out the remains of certain animals out of the submerged land, some of which include lions and mammoths. Some tools and weapons were also recovered.

It must be remembered that part of Plato's description about Atlantis mentioned the presence of elephants. While mammoths are not elephants, a first glance at these two animals bears a close similarity so that one can be easily mistaken for another.

The gradual submersion of Doggerland however is contrary to the stories of Plato. According to him, Atlantis was wiped out in a single day and night, allowing for an instantaneous erasure from the surface of the sea. However, there are those who theorized that although Doggerland slowly sank, its cause of disappearance came after a tsunami triggered by the Storegga Slide. Since it was already low-lying, the tsunami effectively wiped out the area, causing it to sink beneath the waves.

Kumari Kadam

A legend all by itself, Kumari Kadam is a mythical continent that is home to a Tamil civilization. It is supposedly located in the Indian Ocean and was the cradle of civilization. The theory was created when scientists noticed the similarity between India, Madagascar, and Africa. In order to explain these geological similarities, they put forth the possibility of Kumari Kadam, a continent that once built these locations but was eventually divided by the passing of time. Of course, the theory of continental drift was eventually made obsolete and thus the idea of Kumari Kadam was no longer entertained by the scholars. Still, the theory persists in India. It may be likened to Atlantis in that Kumari Kadam is also viewed as a root civilization that eventually disappeared.

Atlantis Is Sweden

In 1679, scientist Olaus Rudbeck put forth the theory that Atlantis exists today as Sweden. He further enlarges the theory by stating that all languages today were developed from the Swedish language, thus making it the "root" form of speech. While his theories are repeated in Sweden, the scientist's theory has been largely ignored and discarded by the rest of the world. It must be noted that Rudbeck himself is Swedish which makes it difficult to believe his theory.

Brasil and Atlantis

Brasil refers to a phantom island which is said to be located in the Atlantic Ocean. While Brasil and Atlantis are two different legends altogether, there are those who believe that the two are one and the same. Brasil is born of Irish myth and according to stories; the island only appears every seven years for just one day. The rest of the time, the island is covered in mist. Accordingly, even if it was seen, Brasil cannot be reached by any form of transportation we have available. The legend of Brasil is largely different from that of Atlantis. The only similarity between the two is that both islands cannot be found and appear to lie beneath the Atlantic Ocean.

Theories on the location of Atlantis have come and gone over the years as science improved in leaps and bounds. As some information comes to light, there are theories that eventually become impossible. For example, Atlantis as a lost continent is now a theory that is largely dismissed as scientists obtain a firmer understanding of tectonic plates and their movements. No doubt however, while some of the locations given above have been firmly dismissed, others are still waiting further research in an effort to prove or disprove the existence of Atlantis within their waters.

Atlantis in Popular Culture

"Popular culture is simpyl a reflection of what the majority seems to want."

- Victor Davis Hanson

A story ripe for further creativity, Atlantis has been the focus of many books, movies, television shows, and music ever since it was reintroduced by Donnelly to the public. While there are still debates on whether Atlantis really existed or not, artists happily took the idea of a lost civilization and ran with it, inputting their own interpretations of Plato's work.

Following are just some of the artistic works inspired by this 9,000 year old island.

Journey to the Center of the Earth

This 1959 film portrayed Atlantis as a city that has sunk so far that it is now located in the center of the earth. Inside, the remains of the lost city can be found.

Cocoon

This 1985 movie made use of extraterrestrial theories by putting forth the concept that Atlantis was the hotbed of aliens some 20,000 years ago. Accordingly, the island was abandoned by the aliens but a few members of their race were left behind during transport.

The Little Mermaid

While Atlantis is not directly mentioned in the movie, it is largely believed that the underwater Kingdom where Ariel lives is Atlantis.

True enough, the king in this Kingdom is Poseidon who is believed to be the owner of Atlantis, according to Greek Mythology.

Atlantis: The Lost Empire

One of the most popular Atlantis film to date, this movie was produced in 2001 and makes use of many of Cayce's ideas for Atlantis. In the movie, above-world explorers managed to find Atlantis and saw a city that is thriving with many of its residents still alive and happily living while detached with the rest of the world. The movie integrates Aztec culture into the Atlanteans while at the same time adding the use of futuristic ships and aircrafts. As per Cayce, this cartoon version of Atlantis uses an energy crystal to power their world.

Doctor Who

One of the longest running televisions shows today, Doctor who has tackled the story of Atlantis three times, each one presenting a different look on how and why it disappeared. During the run of the Second Doctor, it was revealed that while a large part of Atlantis was destroyed thousands of years ago, a portion of it remains in present time.

Of course, those are just some of the most prominent takes of Atlantis in popular culture. These versions have been adapted from current theories with their creators adding or subtracting certain elements to meet their satisfaction. For the most part however, there are certain elements of the Atlantis legend that is the same throughout. It is largely accepted that they are a superior civilization with a knowledge base that is far more than their contemporaries 9,000 years ago.

Even children's cartoons like Spongebob Squarepants have poked fun into the legend of Atlantis, putting their own spin into this mythical island in pursuit of creativity. The main take away however is the fact that Atlantis continues to provide popular culture with inspiration to create, develop, and add more to the legend. Aside from movies, books, and television, Atlantis has also inspired paintings and even music in one form or another.

Atlantis in Greek Mythology

"It did remind me of something out of Greek mythology – the richest king who gets everything he wants, but ultimately his family has a curse on it from the Gods."

-Martin Scorsese

At this point, it becomes important to view Atlantis as it was told in relation to Greek Mythology. As previously discussed, the island was under the protection of Poseidon who originally built the city in tribute to a moral woman named Cleito. On this city, he made a hill in honor of his wife who gave birth to his sons. There were ten in all with Cleito giving birth to twins five times. Eventually, this hill was where the palace of Atlantis was built and where the 10 kings of the city resided to keep the peace. The oldest of the sons was called Atlas, thus the name of the Atlantic Ocean.

Poseidon, as most gods will, laid down rules that the citizens of Atlantis are bound to follow. For a long time, the city flourished and prospered under the guidance of Poseidon. Later on however, the old laws were forgotten and the people of Atlantis succumbed to immoral acts, discarding their respect of the gods and choosing their personal pleasure above that of pleasing Poseidon.

It is for this reason that Atlantis was struck down, barraged by natural disasters so that in a single day and night, the island sank in the bottom of the ocean.

Prior to this disaster however, Atlanteans took the time to build huge structures to honor Poseidon. His sons in particular, created statues of him made purely in gold. In this statue, Poseidon was riding his chariot that is being pulled by horses with wings. Said statue was placed in a temple that was built so high, its topmost portion split the sky.

What's interesting about this city is that they are rich enough that trading with other cities is not necessary. No doubt well provided for by Poseidon, the city grew its own fruits and vegetables, fished from an abundant sea, and hunted for meat in a very prosperous forest. Their vast richness is rivaled only by their advanced culture. It is said that the Atlanteans have a concept of language during their time. They have also mastered architecture due to the various monuments constructed within the city. As per Plato's account, waterways connect this circled city, which brings to mind knowledge of how to build dams and aqueducts. One of the hobbies of citizens of Atlantis was the creation of crystals, which leads to the conclusion that they have some form of alchemy, chemistry, or another form of advanced science in their arsenal.

The people who lived in Atlantis aren't just rich however – they're also bigger than the typical human today. Being ruled by the sons of Poseidon, it stands to reason that many of the Atlanteans are demigods and thus bigger than mortal men.

Building Atlantis

The concentric circles of Atlantis wasn't found this way however, as per stories of Plato. Accordingly, the mountain was carved into by Poseidon where the palace was eventually built. This palace was enclosed in three moats, each one separated by a strip of land. In order to connect these islands with each other, bridges were built spanning the diameter of the circle, allowing citizens of each land to visit others. Canals to the sea were also made, allowing boats to pass right through the islands, allowing for better fishing. Since stories suggest that the Atlanteans did not engage in trade, it can be said that they survived largely on fishing.

The city was well guarded with gates and guards that are posted in every possible entrance. Towers were also constructed, allowing the Atlanteans an extensive view of anything that might be approaching their secured location. Walls were built made of white, black, and red rocks. The precious metal orichalcum covers the said walls.

Other Mysterious Civilizations that Disappeared

"If we open a quarrel between the past and present, we shal find that we have lost the future."

-Winston Churchill

Given that numerous theories on Atlantis have been proven false or are still insufficient for a solid proof, enthusiasts have no problem insinuating that certain civilizations or islands are actually the lost city of Atlantis. At this stage, it is unclear whether even the description given by Plato is accurate or whether scholars can easily discard some of the described characteristics in favor of their own theory.

As it stands however, Atlantis is practically a byword for a lost ancient civilization that disappeared overnight. Following this mindset, practically all mysteriously lost ancient civilizations have been theorized as the inspiration for the Atlantis mentioned by Plato.

That being said, following are famous civilizations that mysterious disappeared and thus have been linked with Atlantis at one time or another:

The Mayans

Many of Donnelly's citations for his book were inspired from Mayan culture. Since they're nowhere near the sea, theories about the Mayan civilization merely cite them as a possible evidence of Atlanteans post-disaster. Accordingly, Atlanteans who survived the wrath of the natural disaster managed to reach Central America and taught the Mayans technology that allowed them to build great structures that last until today. This civilization existed during the first millennium of the AD. With many of their tools surviving today, archeologists have surmised that the Mayans had a concept of math, writing, and even a calendar that is accurate up until this day. They survived with the use of terrace farms and created agricultural feats the supported their way of life. Accordingly, the Mayans started to decline in numbers due to climate change although this is not entirely proven.

Easter Island

You've probably seen the Easter Island Heads, but the people who built them are pretty much still a mystery. Building giant architectures, not to mention the humongous statues lining up the coast of the island, there's no question that this lost civilization is a little too advanced for their time. Said to be a Polynesian civilization, there's no sure reason why they people who built these stunning statues have vanished virtually overnight. One theory however is that the original civilization is composed of voyagers who traveled from island to island. Despite the excellence of their lifestyle, their way of life is not sustainable and thus led to their eventual collapse.

Angkor Wat

Angkor Wat is located in Cambodia and is considered to be one of the largest ancient cities today. It was estimated that Angkor Wat contained more than a million people during its peak, making it akin to a metropolis or a mega city in today's time. It's not exactly known how this amazing civilization died out, but evidence of their existence showed that residents of Angkor Wat were ahead of their time. A thriving hive from 1000 to 1200 AD, the city contains various roads and canals that connected different parts of the civilization. This might well meet the waterways as described by Plato.

Olmec Civilization

The Olmec Civilization is said to be older than the Mayans and the Aztecs. They are best known for the giant heads created by members of the city. They represent a form of amazing architectural feat that has baffled scientists up until today. Even now, it is unknown how these heads were created and why they were created by the Olmecs.

Further proof of their advance knowledge includes their ability to terraform specific regions. A good example would be the San Lorenzo plateau which even now is still considered an architectural wonder.

Indus Valley

This one is located across the expanse of India, Iran, Afghanistan, and Pakistan. This supposes that the Indus Valley civilization is large and wide reaching. In fact, scholars believe that during its peak, the city is home to more than 5 million people, making it one of the biggest settlements of the ancient world. Studies have also shown that they had access to great knowledge, allowing them to build sophisticated forms of structure to facilitate the smooth movement of their city. Among this includes multistory houses, large monuments, and even roadside drainage. Their sudden loss is largely blamed on weather changes, causing an unbearable environment that made it difficult for the citizens to live, plant, and sustain themselves in their land.

While some of these cities have stories of their own and therefore cannot be mistaken for Atlantis, they are excellent proof that a systemized and intelligent form of civilization existed long before what we originally believe. Their existence rewrites history and leaves room for further changes. After all, if these advanced civilizations more ancient than Rome and Egypt existed, why wouldn't there be another that lays claim to an older existence? Atlantis is now the byword for such ancient civilization.

Conclusion

So what is the truth when it comes to the legend of Atlantis? The general consensus is that it does not exist and was simply created by Plato to prove a point. However, we live in a world where new discoveries are made every day. The likelihood of Atlantis coming to surface in the distant future therefore is always a probability that scientists contemplate in the course of their explorations of the world in general.

Today, the main template used for Atlantis is the writings of Plato for the simple reason that he is the first person to refer to the lost city. Documents that evidence Atlantis, however, may be found in later writings which should help narrow down the search for this legendary location.

As of now, the civilizations found while searching for Atlantis deserve their own spot in history. While the Minoans, the Eastern Island civilization, or the Mayans may not have been Atlantis – their culture bears study, preservation, and retelling.

As for Atlantis, the mere fact that no concrete proof exists to solidify its reality, this should not stop scholars from further exploring the possibility of an actual Atlantis as described by Plato. At the very least, more civilizations will be discovered that are not Atlantis, but are every bit as important in today's history.

Printed in Great Britain
by Amazon